STEP ONE:
Play Flute

by Hal Archer

**Master the basics as you step into the exciting world of playing the flute.
A complete and proven method that includes over thirty classical and folk tunes
to play and enjoy as you learn.**

Amsco Publications
New York/London/Paris/Sydney/Copenhagen/Berlin/Tokyo/Madrid

Cover photography by Randall Wallace
Project editor: Peter Pickow
Interior design and layout: Len Vogler

Order No. AM 974358
US International Standard Book Number: 0.8256.2727.3
UK International Standard Book Number: 0.7119.9473.0

Exclusive Distributors:
Music Sales Corporation
257 Park Avenue South, New York, NY 10010 USA
Music Sales Limited
8/9 Frith Street, London W1D 3JB England
Music Sales Pty. Limited
120 Rothschild Street, Rosebery, Sydney, NSW 2018, Australia

Printed in the United States of America by
Vicks Lithograph and Printing Corporation

Contents

Introduction

So you've dreamed of playing the flute, but are a little afraid of getting started. Well, with a little study and practice, you can do it. This introductory flute method is easy and fun, and gives you all the skills you need to continue learning hundreds of songs on your own, or with a teacher.

The *transverse,* or horizontal, flute has been in use for several hundred years, but vertical flutes date back to ancient civilizations and even prehistory. Today most transverse flutes are made of metal, but in the early days they were made of wood. Because of this, the flute is a member of the woodwind family of instruments. Today, the flute is one of the most popular instruments in the world. Besides the *concert C flute,* there are also the *alto flute, bass flute, contrabass flute,* and *piccolo.*

Whether you intend to be a professional flute player, or simply wish to play for your community, family, and friends—this book is for you. So, get ready to learn the basics of flute as you play some of the world's most popular melodies.

Flute Basics

Range of the Modern Flute

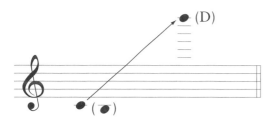

Parts of the Flute

headjoint

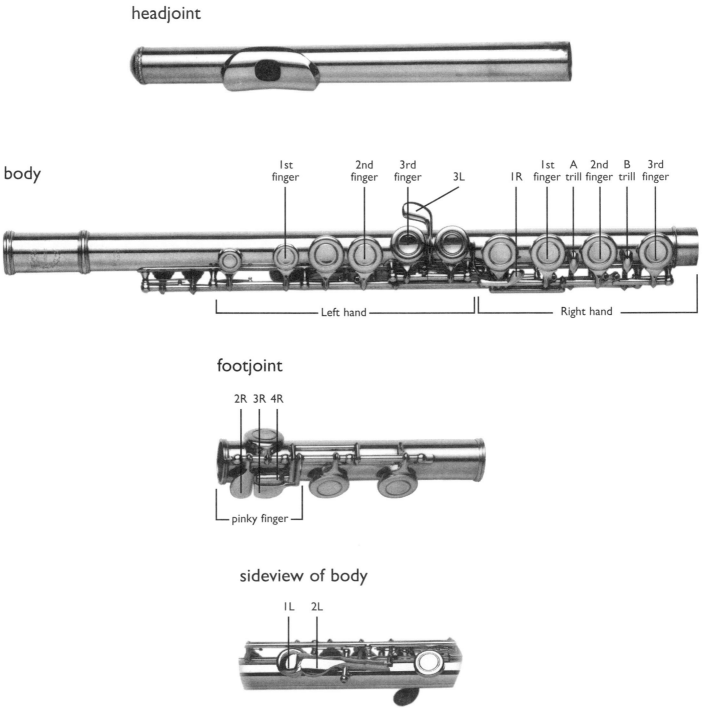

body

1st finger   2nd finger   3rd finger   3L   1R   1st finger   A trill   2nd finger   B trill   3rd finger

Left hand   Right hand

footjoint

2R 3R 4R

pinky finger

sideview of body

1L   2L

Caring for Your Flute

Putting your flute together carefully is very important. Using a little pressure and a twisting motion join the ends onto the middle section. This should be done without squeezing or touching the key sections. Do not push the headjoint all the way in, as you may later want to adjust it for tuning. When you have finished twisting, be sure that all finger holes of the foot and middle are in a straight line and that the hole of the headjoint is also in line.

Cleaning Your Flute

If you always make sure to clean the ends of the sections before you play, your flute will assemble easily. Grease should not be used.

After playing, use the cleaning rod with a clean cotton cloth to swab the insides of the flute thoroughly. It is also a good idea to wipe the exterior of the flute so that dirt and perspiration do not destroy the metal's shiny surface.

Never adjust or remove the top round cap of your flute.

Holding Your Flute

1. Place the flute on your lap with the headjoint on the left. You will see keys 1L/2L facing up.

2. Put your left thumb on keys 1L/2L perpendicular to the flute.

3. Put your right thumb under the keys 1 and 2 of the right hand and your little finger (pinky) on 2R.

4. Maintaining this position lift the flute with a rolling motion towards your lips. (Your left wrist should be slightly squared, with the palm and wrist joint outside the body of the flute.)

5. Check yourself in the mirror.

Front view of hands
Hands are relaxed; wrists drooped; fingers curved over the keys, lightly resting on or close to keys.

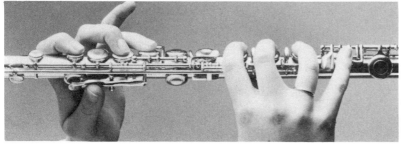

Back view of hands

Making Your First Sound

Before attempting you first sound, try this experiment. Place a rice grain between your lips, holding it in place with minimum pressure. The rice grain shape represents your *blowhole* (*embouchure*). Keeping the lips closed around the rice grain, blow gently so that you don't dislodge the grain. Look at your mouth position in a mirror so that you can make this blowhole every time you play the flute. Remember, the rice grain is the size of the hole you want.

When you are comfortable, take the headjoint, hold it at both ends and place the lip plate in the indentation below your lower lip. Cover approximately half of the hole with the lower lip. Shaping the blowhole the way you practiced with the rice, gently blow air across and slightly under the outer edge of the lip plate hole.

There are two ways to correctly begin these sounds on the flute. One is to blow through your correct blowhole as if to bend the flame of a candle. The second is to place the tip of the tongue behind the front teeth and whisper *tew, tew, tew*. This second way causes a small expulsion of air and is the prefered method.

With this success you are on your way.

Now put your flute together and repeat all these things. Don't let the weight of the flute alter your mouth position.

Monitor Yourself in a Mirror!

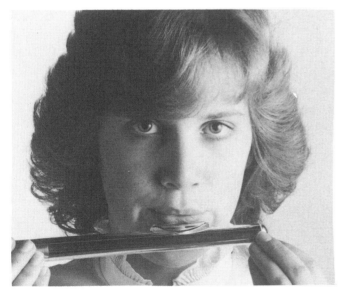
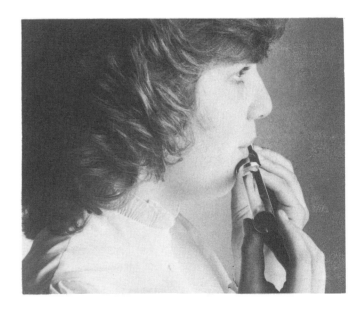

The Signs and Characters of Music

Music is represented on paper by a combination of characters and signs. Symbols called *notes* are written upon and between five lines which is the *staff*.

The sign at the beginning of the staff is called the *treble clef* or *G clef*.

The staff is divided by *barlines* into *bars*, or *measures*, of music as follows:

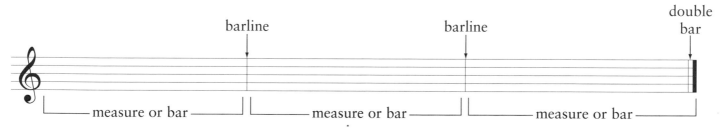

At the end of a song you will see a *double bar*.

At the beginning of the piece of music you will see two numbers. This is called the *time signature* and indicates the number of equal value notes in each bar. The upper number is the beats and the lower number is the note that has one beat.

For example:

Different combinations of notes and rests can be combined in each bar to equal the four quarter-notes indicated by this time signature.

Here are some more basics of music notation:

whole note	o	whole rest	‒	=	4 beats
half note	♩	half rest	‒	=	2 beats
quarter note	♩	quarter rest	𝄽	=	1 beat
eighth note	♪	eighth rest	𝄾	=	½ beat
sixteenth note	♬	sixteenth rest	𝄿	=	¼ beat

A whole note is equivalent to 2 half notes, 4 quarter notes, 8 eighth notes, *etc.*

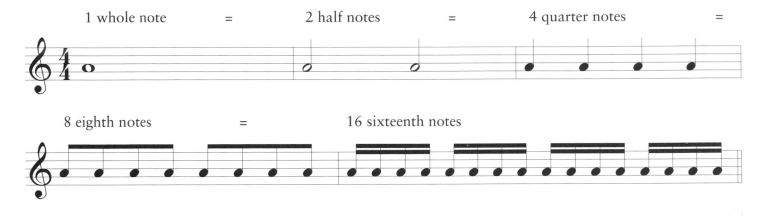

The rhythm is different yet the time taken up is the same.

A dot next to the note (♩·) indicates that one-half of that note's value is to be added to the duration of that note.

For example:

♩·	=	♩	+	♩
♩·	=	♩	+	♪
♪·	=	♪	+	♬

The same principle applies to rests.

‒·	=	‒	+	𝄽
𝄽·	=	𝄽	+	𝄾
𝄾·	=	𝄾	+	𝄿

Naming the Notes

Notes are named by their value in beats or time and by their position on the staff.

The spaces are

F   A   C   E

The lines are

E   G   B   D   F

The combination of lines and spaces makes use of the first seven letters of the alphabet repeated over and over.

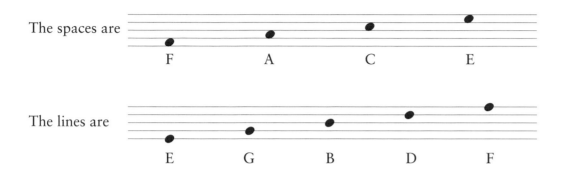

D   E   F   G   A   B   C   D   E   F   G   F   E   D   C   B   A   G   F   E   D

Leger lines: Additional lines are used above and below the staff to extend the range of notes.

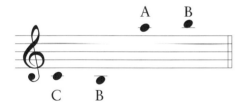

A   B

C   B

Let's Play

Let's play a *whole note* and count four beats:
1-2-3-4.

Here is the fingering for the note B.

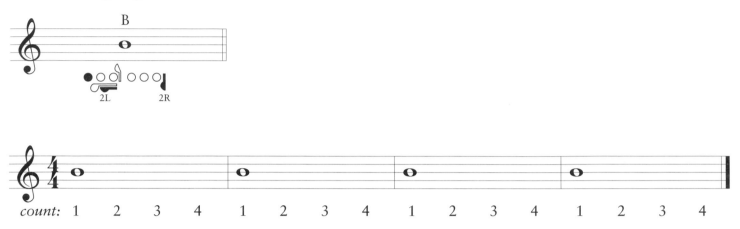

Have you remembered your rice grain? Look in the mirror.

Now repeat it with your tongue behind and above your front teeth saying "tew-tew-tew."

New note A.

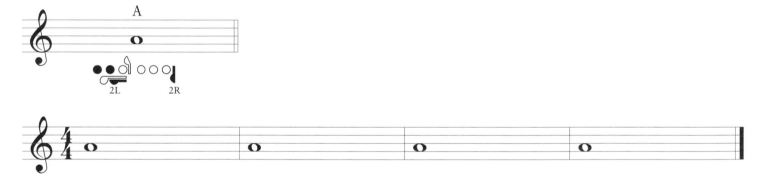

Combining B and A.

New note G.

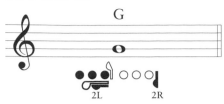

A *whole rest* is four beats of silence.

Let's practice.

Half note = two beats
Half rest = two beats

Music B-A-G

count: 1 2 3 4   1 2 3 4 *etc.*

New Note C.

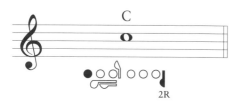

Quarter note = 1 beat
Quarter rest = 1 beat

count: 1　2　3　4　　1　2　3　4　　1　2　3　4　　1　2　3　4

MELODY WITH C

$\frac{2}{4}$ = Two beats in each measure, and a quarter note gets one beat.

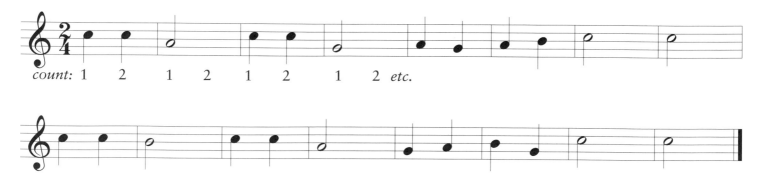

count: 1　2　1　2　1　2　1　2 *etc.*

New note D.

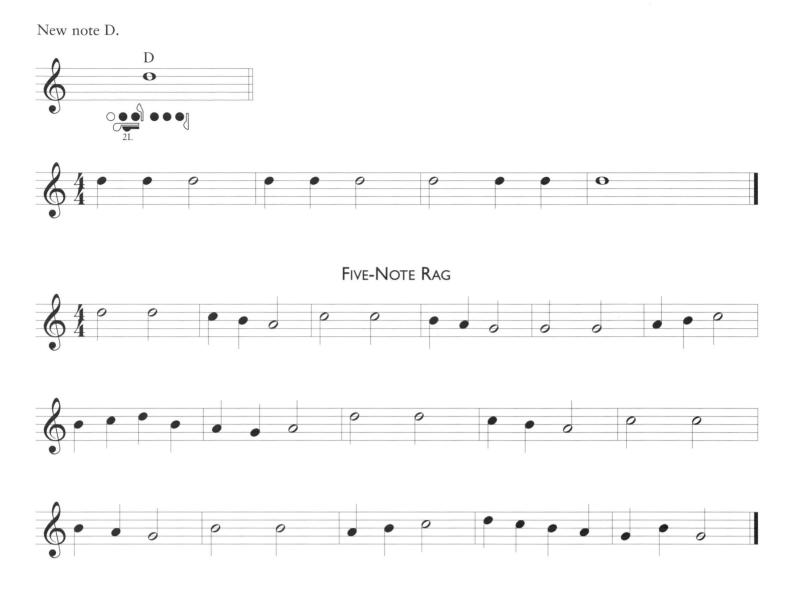

FIVE-NOTE RAG

$\frac{3}{4}$ = Three beats in each measure, and a quarter note gets one beat.

ROSES FROM THE SOUTH

Johann Strauss

count: 1 2 3 1 2 3 1 2 3 1 2 3 1 2 3 etc.

tie

A *tie* (‿) joins two notes of the same pitch. Play them with one breath.

Practice Two

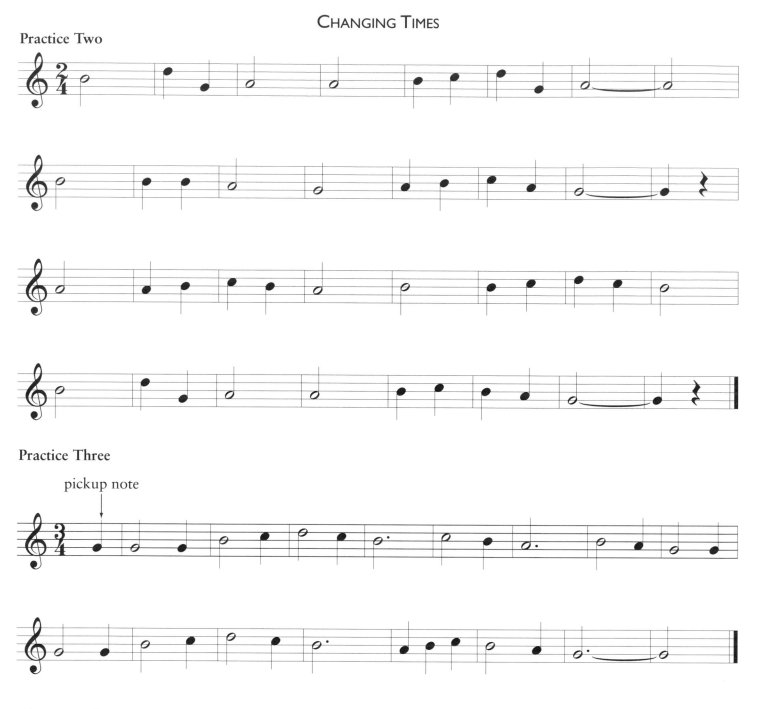

Practice Three

pickup note

The time value of a *pickup note* is borrowed from the last bar of the piece.

Practice Four

New note F#.

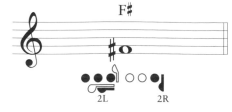

A *sharp sign* (♯) raises the pitch one-half step.

F♯ Melody

LIGHTLY ROW
(duet)

Traditional

The sharp sign (♯) in now next to the treble clef. This is called a
key signature. It means that every F should be played as F♯.

key signature

À La Classical

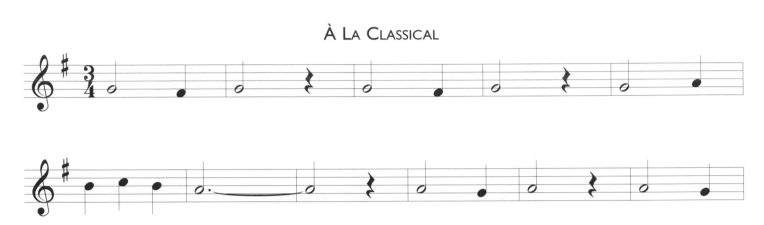

One eighth note has the time value of one-half of a quarter note.

Two eighth notes have the time value of one quarter note.

An eighth note rest indicates a half beat of silence.

count: 1 and 2 and 3   4   1   2 and 3   4   1 and 2 and 3   4   1   2 and 3   4

MARCH

count: 1 and 2 and 1 and 2 1 and 2 and 1 and 2 etc.

New note E.

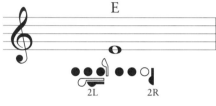

For quick success, blow down into the flute's blowhole a little
more without forcing the air.

A *slur* (⌢) connects two or more notes played without using the
tongue to separate them. Simply change fingers while blowing one
airsteam.

JADE WINTER

SECRET AGENT MAN

The coordination involved in changing from E to F♯ needs special attention. Practice the finger motion without playing until you are comfortable, and be sure your little finger stays down.

:‖ = Repeat the song from the beginning.

THE WANDERER

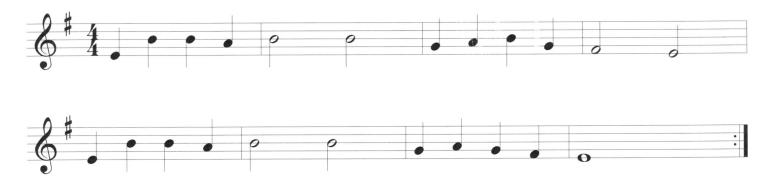

New note D.

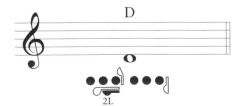

Slowly

A dot under or over a note means to play it *staccato*, or very short. The dash means you should give the note its full value.

OLD MAC

Traditional

GOOD KING WENCESLAS

English

A dotted quarter note (♩.) is usually followed by an eighth note. The dot is equal to half the value of the quarter note (♩. = ♩ ♪).

ODE TO JOY

Ludwig van Beethoven

21

New note F.

SHORTNIN' BREAD

A good way to play staccato notes is to change the way you use
your tongue. Say "tewt-tewt-tewt-tewt."

New note C.

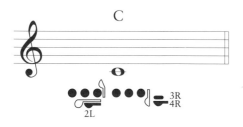

This C is written on a leger line below the staff.

The $\frac{4}{4}$ time signature is often written as 𝄴.

The Caissons

Edward Gruber

March

A *major scale* is made up of eight notes ascending and descending in alphabetical order. It has a unique sound, and begins and ends on the same letter name.

C Major Scale

JOY TO THE WORLD

George Frideric Handel

Allegro (Lively)

New note E.

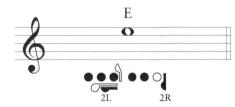

To play this E, slide the lower jaw forward just slightly. Continue to blow toward the outer edge of the flute's blowhole.

Practice these *octaves*.

WALTZ

D.C. al Fine

D.C. = *Da Capo*
Go back to the beginning and play until the *Fine* (end).

New note B♭.

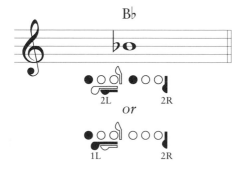

A *flat sign* (♭) lowers a note by one half step. It may be placed next to the note or in the key signature, just like the sharp sign.

Most of the notes you have played up to now have alternate fingerings just like the B♭. For instance, the D and F notes in "Au Clair de la Lune" may be fingered with the 1L key instead of the 2L key. Using these fingerings makes it easier to use the second, simpler B♭ fingering above. You can explore alternate fingerings by referring to the Fingering Chart in the back of this book.

Au Clair de la Lune

French

’ = take a breath

The Saints

American

Arpeggios

An *arpeggio* is a series of notes that outline a chord. Notice how the arpeggios below are created by playing every other note of the scale.

New note F.

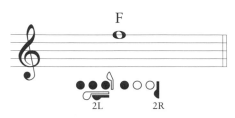

F Major Scale

F Arpeggio

Practice this at first using the tongue on each note and later slurring each bar. Aim for clear, clean note changes, and keep your air going when you slur. Remember your jaw slide and of course your lips.

Arpeggios on the Chords of the F Scale

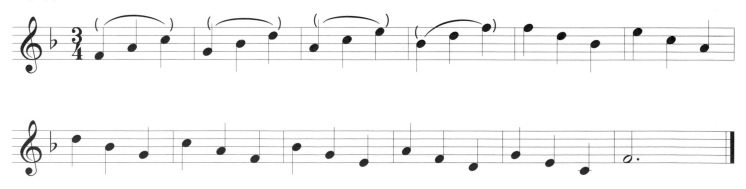

Waltzing Matilda

Australian

Marines Hymn

Special Endings

When a composer wants to repeat a section of music but wants a different ending the second time through, he or she writes this for the musician.

| 1. Play this the first time. | | 2. Play this the second time (after you have repeated the section of music). |

EXERCISE IN C

A round is a song for two or more people. When the first person gets as far as ②, the second person begins to play.

WHITE CORAL BELLS
(ROUND)

As you play your next new note, you will need to balance the flute using four things:

    1. the side of your left index finger near the knuckle,

    2. your right thumb,

    3. your right pinky, and

    4. your lower lip.

If you push your right hand forward slightly, you will feel the pressure of the flute below your bottom lip. Make sure that your flute is balanced before you blow.

New note C#.

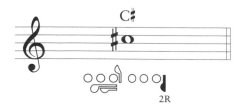

D Major Scale (Using F# and C#)

O GOD, BENEATH THY GUIDING HAND

Traditional

LULLABY

Johannes Brahms

Remember...

AMERICA THE BEAUTIFUL

Samuel A. Ward

New note F#.

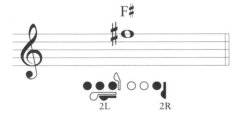

Remember to keep your lips close together and your jaw forward.

À la Mozart

Wolfgang Amadeus Mozart

—— —— —— = Long full notes with your tongue saying *da-da-da*.

Legato Melody

Polka

Czechoslovakian

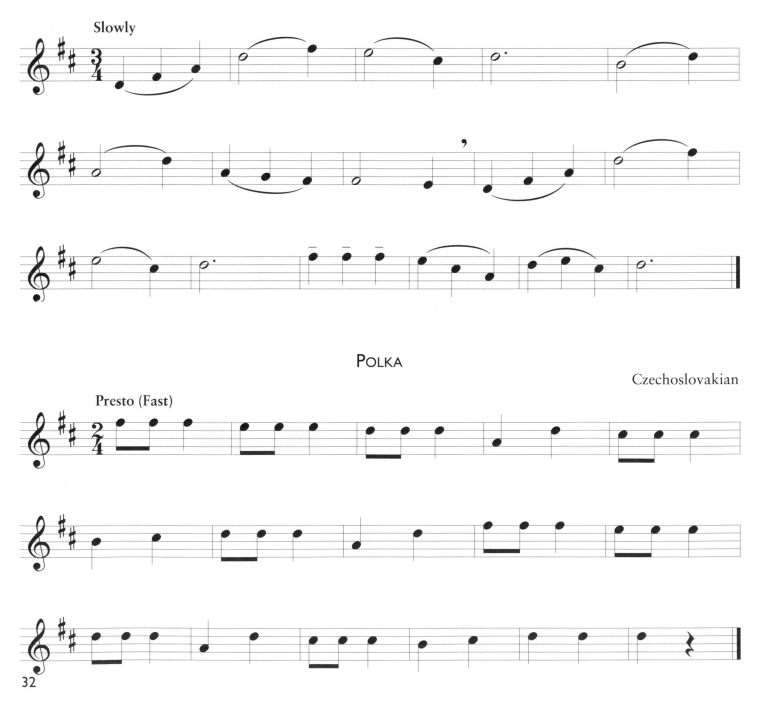

New note G.

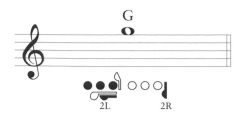

HOME ON THE RANGE

American

DRINK TO ME ONLY WITH THINE EYES

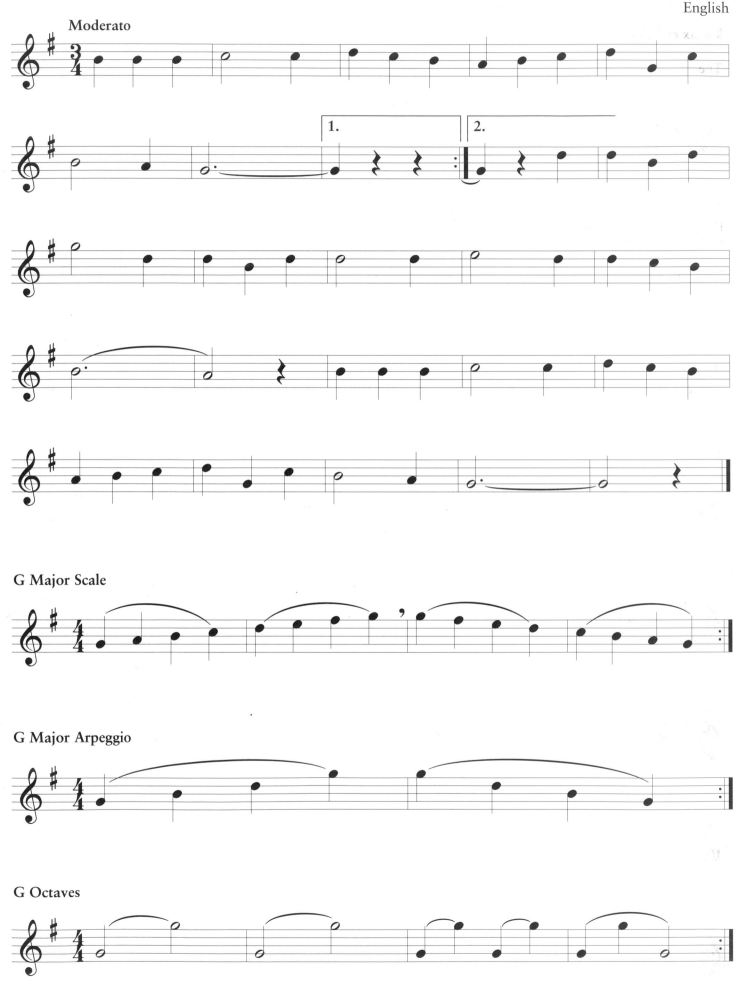

G Major Scale

G Major Arpeggio

G Octaves

A New Time Signature

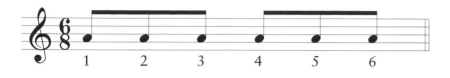 = six eighth-notes in a bar.

The six eighth-notes are most often written in two groups of three.

This grouping gives the feeling of two strong beats with three little parts. Try counting like this *1, 2, 3 — 4, 5, 6.* Do this several times in a row and you will get the feeling.

This will now change the way eighth notes are used and will also make it necessary to use the following kinds of notation:

The G Major Scale in Time

New note A.

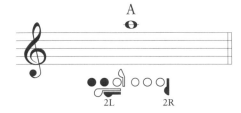

BLOW THE MAN DOWN

English

MARCH

D.C. al Fine

MULBERRY BUSH

English

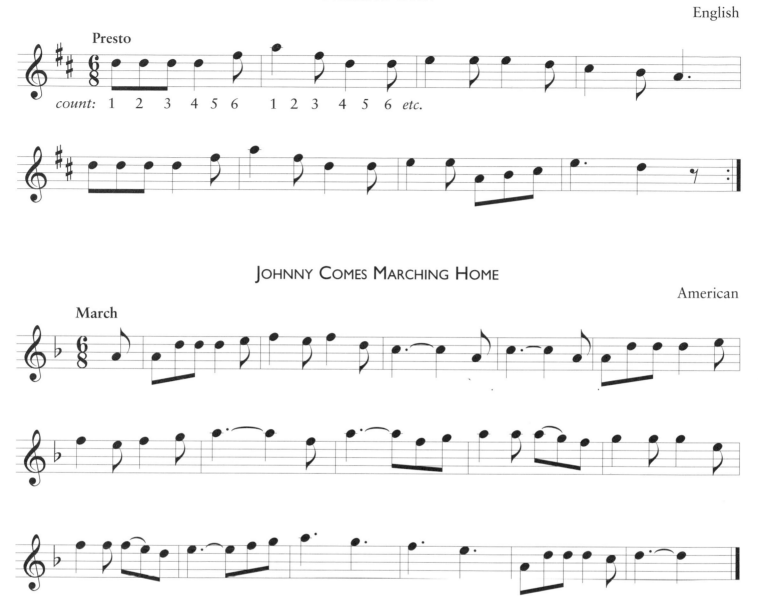

Presto

count: 1 2 3 4 5 6   1 2 3 4 5 6 etc.

JOHNNY COMES MARCHING HOME

American

March

Dynamics

The use of *dynamics* helps to bring out the feeling of the music.

Dynamic markings

p	=	*piano*, soft
mp	=	*mezzo piano*, medium soft
mf	=	*mezzo forte*, medium loud
f	=	*forte*, loud
<	=	*crescendo*, get gradually louder
>	=	*diminuendo*, get gradually softer
>	=	*accent mark*, emphasize the note

To play louder or softer, you simply increase or decrease the amount of air you are blowing. You may notice that the pitch changes a bit the harder or softer you blow; adjust your embouchure and listen—the right pitch will return.

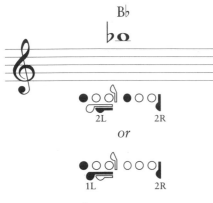

New note B♭.

ADAGIO IN B♭

SILENT NIGHT

Vive la Compagnie

French

New note E♭.

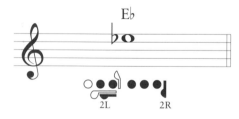

E♭

2L   2R

America
(My Country 'Tis of Thee)

English

Frère Jacques is a four-part round with a new part entering every four measures. To play along with the CD, you should come in second; that is, start playing when the first player reaches the number 2. Then play the tune four times through.

FRÈRE JACQUES
(ROUND)

French

B♭ Major Scale (Using B♭ and E♭)

A *fermata* (𝄐) means hold the note a little longer. We call it a "bird's eye" for short.

B♭ Major Arpeggio

A natural sign (♮) placed before a note cancels a sharp or flat that has occurred earlier in the measure or is in the key signature. In measure 9 of the Christmas carol below, the natural sign before the E note cancels the E♭ in the key signature.

It Came upon the Midnight Clear

Richard Storrs Willis

New note B.

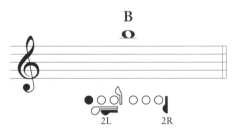

Remember to slide your lower jaw forward just slightly. Don't put any pressure on your lower lip. Also remember your rice-grain blowhole.

New note C.

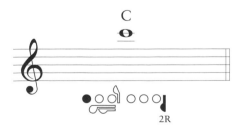

In order to get C after B, maintain the same lip and jaw positions and lift your left thumb off of the 2L key just slightly. Balance the flute by applying a little pressure from the left index finger, but keep the right thumb and pinky in place.

Two-Octave C Major Scale

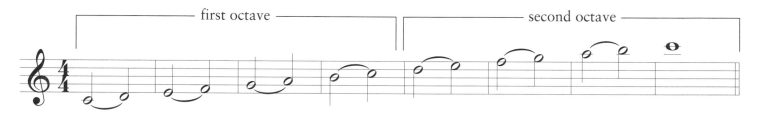

C Major Arpeggio Practice

THE KERRY DANCERS

New note C#.

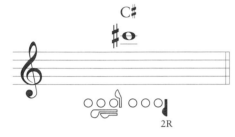

Keep the flute balanced, as described on the previous page.

New note D.

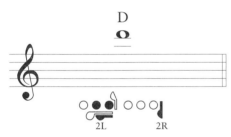

Practice this scale and arpeggio both tongued and slurred.

Two-Octave D Major Scale

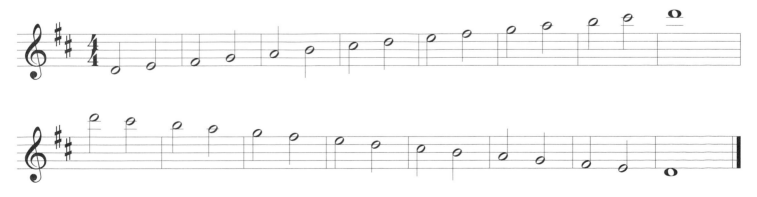

D Major Arpeggio

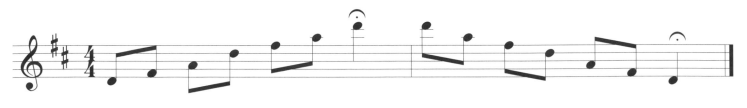

THE ASH GROVE

English

Andante (Walking tempo)

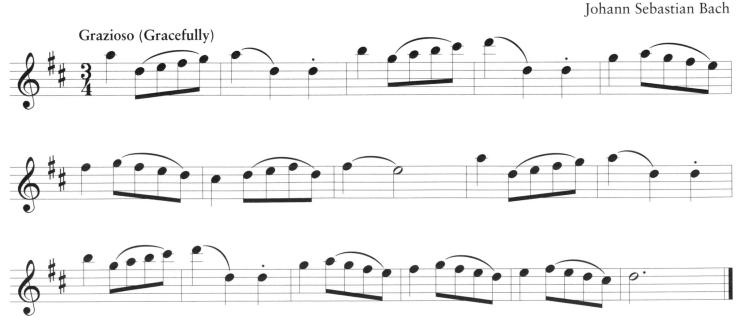

Fine

D.C. *al Fine*

MINUET

Johann Sebastian Bach

Grazioso (Gracefully)

Compact Disc Track Listing

1. Introduction
2. First Note: B
3. B-Note Exercise
4. New Note: A
5. A-Note Exercise
6. B-to-A Exercise
7. New Note: G
8. G-Note Exercise
9. B, A, and G Exercise
10. *Music B-A-G*
11. New Note: C and C-Note Exercise
12. *Melody with C*
13. ⅜ Exercise
14. New Note: D and D-Note Exercise
15. *Five-Note Rag*
16. *Roses from the South*
17. *Changing Times: Practice Two*
18. *Changing Times: Practice Three*
19. *Changing Times: Practice Four*
20. New Note: F♯
21. *F♯ Melody*
22. *Lightly Row* (duet)
23. *À la Classical*
24. Eighth-Note Exercise
25. *March*
26. New Note: E and E-Note Exercise
27. *Jade Winter*
28. *Secret Agent Man*
29. *The Wanderer*
30. New Note: D and D-Note Exercise
31. *Old Mac*
32. *Good King Wenceslas*
33. *Ode to Joy*
34. New Note: F and F-Note Exercise
35. *Shortnin' Bread*
36. New Note: C and C-Note Exercise
37. *The Caissons*
38. C Major Scale
39. *Joy to the World*
40. New Note: E and E-Note Octave Exercise
41. *Waltz*
42. New Note: B♭
43. *Au Clair de la Lune*
44. *The Saints*
45. New Note: F
46. F Major Scale
47. F Arpeggio
48. Arpeggios on the Chords of the F Scale
49. *Waltzing Matilda*
50. *Marines Hymn*
51. *Exercise in C*
52. *White Coral Bells*
53. New Note: C♯
54. D Major Scale
55. *O God, Beneath Thy Guiding Hand*
56. *Lullaby*
57. *America the Beautiful*
58. New Note: F♯
59. *À la Mozart*
60. *Legato Melody*
61. *Polka*
62. New Note: G
63. *Home on the Range*
64. *Drink to Me Only with Thine Eyes*
65. G Major Scale
66. G Major Arpeggio
67. G-Note Octave Exercise
68. G Major Scale in ⅜ Time
69. New Note: A
70. *Blow the Man Down*
71. *March*
72. *Mulberry Bush*
73. *Johnny Comes Marching Home*
74. New Note: B♭
75. *Adagio in B♭*
76. *Silent Night*
77. *Vive la Compagnie*
78. New Note: E♭
79. *America (My Country 'Tis of Thee)*
80. *Frère Jacques* (round)
81. B♭ Major Scale
82. B♭ Major Scale with Fermata
83. B♭ Major Arpeggio
84. *It Came upon the Midnight Clear*
85. New Note: B
86. New Note: C
87. B-to-C Exercise
88. Two-Octave C Major Scale
89. C Major Arpeggio Practice
90. *The Kerry Dancers*
91. New Note: C♯
92. New Note: D
93. Two-Octave D Major Scale and Arpeggio
94. *The Ash Grove*
95. *Minuet*
96. Afterword

Fingering Chart

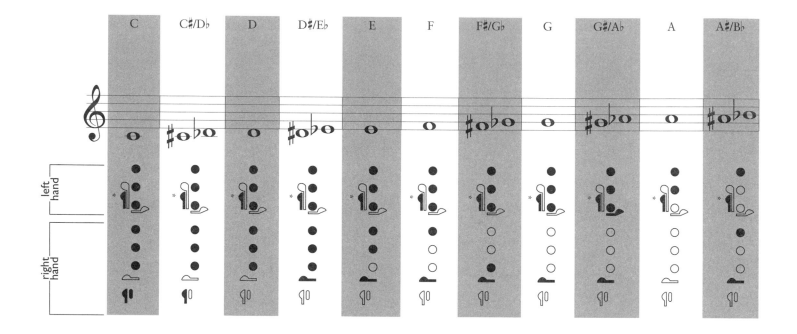

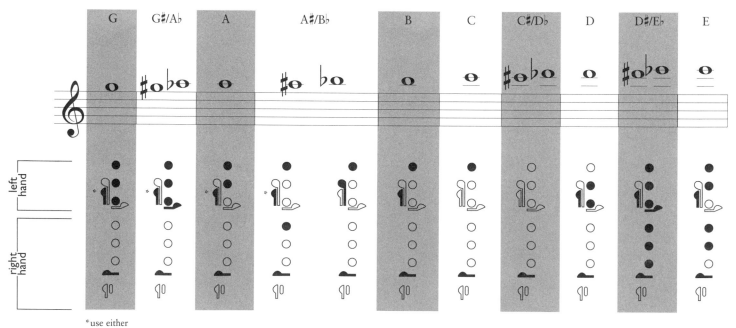

*use either
2L or 1L key

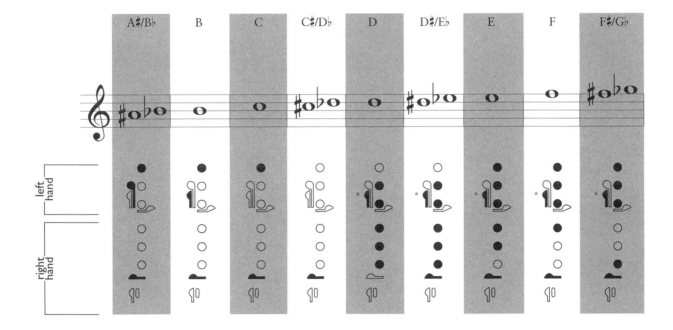

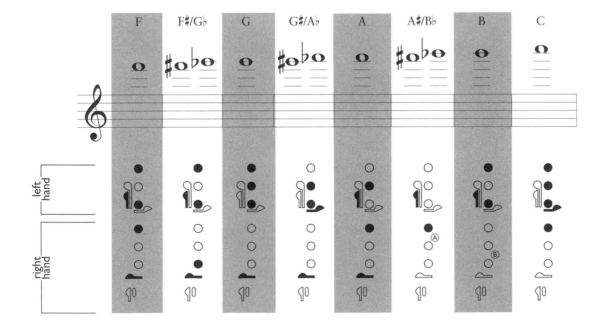

About the Author

Hal Archer is an internationally recognized flutist and educator. In a concert career that has spanned over twenty-five years, Mr. Archer has played with such notable ensembles as the English Chamber Orchestra, the New York City Ballet, the Festival Orchestra (Spoletto, Italy), the Alvin Ailey Dance Company, the New York Lyric Opera, and Les Nouveaux Jongleurs Trio. He divides his time between Welland, Ontario, and Barbados, West Indies.